Kids' Garden Adventure

Kids' Garden Adventure

DON BURKE

Activities

Making and Creating 60

Introduction

Welcome to adventure in the garden! This book is for adventurous kids. It's full of challenging and creative experiments and projects that are great fun to do.

Most projects can be completed using ordinary household objects plus seeds, gravel and potting mix.

We suggest that you go through this book, picking out two or three projects that you think will be real fun to begin with.

Then write a list of the things that you will need to get started: for example, potting mix, special packets of seed, food colouring or even an old aquarium. This may mean a shopping trip to the local garden centre or plant nursery. Some rare seeds may have to be ordered online if local garden centres don't stock them. We've also included a list of suppliers for you at the back.

Other projects like making seedpod creatures may mean that you go on a scavenging hunt around the local parks and gardens looking for strange seedpods.

You can go on adventures looking for moss growing on stone walls, on sidewalks or even in the lawn in shady areas. The moss collected is perfect for moss gardens or for use on top of a bonsai potting mix.

There are some scientific projects too, such as finding the ultraviolet colours in plant flowers. For this you will need a UV mini torch. We also have an experiment on how to change the colours of flowers.

Along the way you will develop skills in growing baby plants from seeds or cuttings: this is called plant propagation. You will also learn how to grow bonsai plants, how to grow a vegetable garden and how to design a garden around a house from nothing.

All of these projects were developed by qualified horticulturists and, if done carefully following the instructions, they all work! The projects are fun to do as well.

We really hope that you enjoy the projects and look forward to hearing from you. Our address is at the back of this book.

Items You Will Need

TROWEL
Use a trowel to dig and plant seeds with. You will use one for many of the projects in this book.

COMPASS AND THERMOMETER
A compass can be used to find the sunniest spot in your garden. It is important to know this because most plants grow better when they get more light, and there are only some that like the shade. The amount of sunlight in your garden will also vary with the seasons.

Take a compass and hold it flat in the palm of your hand and turn your whole body until the end of the compass needle is pointing to north.

If you are in the southern hemisphere, you will get more sun in the north facing part of your garden, and if you are in the northern hemisphere you will get more sun in the south facing part of your garden.

A thermometer can be used to see how hot or cold it is on any given day.

UV (ULTRAVIOLET) MINI TORCH
When people see colours in normal light, known as visible light, they see them in a spectrum of red, orange, yellow, green blue and violet. A UV (ultraviolet) torch produces ultraviolet light that allows you to see UV fluorescence.

Many plants, flowers, animals and insects have UV colours (fluorescent parts) on them that we humans can't see in normal light. But many birds and insects can see them. A UV torch allows you to see part of what they see! Using it can reveal hidden UV colours on flowers that some plants produce to attract insects to pollinate them. Follow the instructions in the Invisible UV Colours activity.

Growing and Exploring

Creating life is the most fun thing that you can do! In this chapter, you will find out how to use honey (yes, honey!) to help cuttings from plants to sprout roots and grow into new living plants.

These new plants make great gifts for friends or you can sell them at fairs or fetes to raise money for good causes.

You can also grow a new pineapple from the green top that most people throw away. Or you can raid the kitchen cupboards or the refrigerator and grow garlic or avocados in your garden.

Professional gardeners use greenhouses to grow plants, but you can use an old clear plastic soft drink bottle or an old clear plastic bag.

When you grow some plants from seeds, magic happens.

Nasturtium seeds produce magical plants with round leaves that make water sit on top of the leaf in a big, round ball! The balls run all over the leaves as you tilt them.

There is also a project on growing snapdragons from seed. Snapdragon seeds produce plants that have monster flowers: flowers that can bite your finger like a beast! ...but it doesn't really hurt.

Plants do really amazing things. Some plants produce ultraviolet (UV) patterns on their flowers. These patterns act like runway lights for aeroplanes – they guide the way for the insect to land on the flower.

You can use a UV mini torch to reveal the hidden UV patterns on the flower, as people normally can't see UV colour.

Magic Nasturtiums

Nasturtiums are easy to grow and their leaves do magical things!
When you splash a drop of water onto a leaf, it turns into a liquid silver ball and slides
around like mercury. This is a great magic trick to show your friends!

1. Buy some nasturtium seeds. If you live in a warm area you can sow your seeds from spring to early autumn, in cooler areas, sow only in spring.

2. Using a trowel, put some seed-raising potting mix in some pots. Make a 2-3cm deep hole with your finger. Drop your seed into the hole and cover with potting mix. Plant several seeds in case some don't come up. You can also sow the seeds directly into garden beds.

3. Water your seeds and place them in a sunny spot. Be sure to water them regularly.

4. Seeds will germinate in about 2-3 weeks and plants start to flower in about 10-12 weeks.

5. Your plants will flower in summer and autumn and come in shades of orange, yellow and red.

6. Water regularly but don't fertilise too much or you won't get many flowers.

did you know: *Nasturtiums are originally from Peru and so grow best in a mild climate. They will not grow well in very cold areas.*

Rating: Medium

You will need:
- Nasturtium seeds
- Seed raising potting mix
- Trowel
- Compass
- Pots

Snapdragon

Grow your own little dragon monsters in your garden. Snapdragons are pretty flowers shaped like a dragon's head and if you squeeze them, their mouths open wide and they'll give you a friendly nip!

1. Buy some dwarf snapdragon seeds. Dwarf snapdragons are available in many colours.

2. Using a trowel, fill a medium sized pot with potting mix and lightly tamp down to level. Scatter the seeds over the surface of the potting mix and press lightly into mix. Snapdragons need light to germinate so there's no need to cover the seeds.

3. Gently spray with a fine mist of water and keep damp until seedlings appear – usually 10 to 14 days.

4. When the seedlings appear the pot can be moved so it gets sun for half the day. After two weeks move into full sun. Check for sunny spots using a compass.

5. When the seedlings have two or three sets of leaves, pinch back the tops and fertilise with a soluble plant food. This will help them to flower better.

6. Expect flowers about 16 weeks after sowing seeds.

> *tip:* When you first plant your seeds keep the potting mix moist by covering the pot with cling wrap or clear plastic until seedlings appear.

Rating: Medium

You will need:

- Dwarf snapdragon (Anthirrhinum) seeds
- Potting mix
- Medium size pot
- Mist sprayer
- Trowel
- Compass

Grow a Free Vegetable Garden

You can create your own free vegetable garden from kitchen scraps. Many plants will grow from the scraps you normally throw away. Here's three you might like to try!

Avocado

1. Get an adult to cut open an avocado and ask them to save the seed for you.

2. Plant the seed, pointy side up into a pot filled with potting mix and water in well.

3. Put your pot in a sunny spot. Water it regularly. The soil should be kept moist but not saturated.

4. Avocados are slow growing. You should see some reasonable growth within a year. Once your seedling is about 30cm tall you can plant it out in the garden. It will need lots of room. Avocados can grow to 20m or more!

5. It will take many years for it to start to fruit. Some avocados grown from seed may never bear fruit.

6. To have the best chance at fruit get two grafted varieties from your nursery. Having two will help with pollination, which means you get fruit!

Garlic

1. Collect what you will need. Quite often garlic will sprout small green shoots while stored in the kitchen.

2. Plant individual cloves 3-5cm deep in a pot filled with potting mix and water in.

3. Place the pot in a sunny spot in autumn or early winter and it will grow into a hand of garlic by the next summer.

4. You can also plant your cloves straight into a vegetable patch.

5. Pick the garlic when the tops of the plants start to wilt and die off.

6. Pull up the whole plant and then hang it up to dry. Garlic should be stored in a spot with good air circulation.

Rating: Easy/Medium

You will need:
- Garlic bulbs
- Large pot or vegetable patch
- Potting mix
- Trowel
- Compass

Pineapple

1. Ask an adult to cut off the leafy end of a pineapple with 3-4cm of fruit attached. Trim the rough edges.

2. Eat the rest of the fruit!

3. Fill the pot with potting mix almost to the top.

4. Place the trimmed piece in the potting mix, covering up the attached fruit so that all you can see are the leaves emerging from the potting mix.

5. Moisten and place in a warm spot in full sun. Keep the potting mix lightly moist.

6. It will take about two years for a pineapple to form. It will take less time if you live in the tropics.

Rating: Easy/Medium

You will need:

- Pineapple top with leaves attached
- Pot
- Potting mix
- Trowel
- Compass

Mini Greenhouse

It is very easy to make your own mini greenhouse, which will help you to grow cuttings (see Striking Cuttings Activity). The mini greenhouse keeps humidity around your cuttings to encourage them to make roots and grow well when they are young.

1. If your pot is small, you can simply cut a large soft plastic drink bottle in half to make your greenhouse. You may need to ask an adult for help. Squeezing the bottle in the middle makes it easy to cut.

2. Both halves can be turned upside down and placed over the cuttings in pots creating a greenhouse.

3. Another method you can use for any size of pot is using a wire coat hanger

as a frame with a plastic bag over it. First, stretch a coat hanger and bend the hook end straight and stick it in your pot; be careful of your plant.

4. Slide a large clear plastic bag over the frame.

5. Use a rubber band or a tie to secure the bag to the pot.

6. Always place cuttings in a brightly lit spot but not full sun.

tip: *Seedlings as well as cuttings can be started in the greenhouse. You can also untwist the hook end of your coat hanger and stick both ends of the wire into opposite sides of the pot for greater stability.*

Striking Cuttings

Many plants will grow from a piece of stem cut from the parent plant. Easy plants to try are: lavender, rosemary, coleus, begonia, pelargoniums and geraniums, camellias, azaleas and buxus. Learn to take cuttings and you can grow many garden plants for free! We used rosemary.

1. Take cuttings using scissors or secateurs 7-10cm (4in) long from the ends of healthy top growth that does not have a flower, flower bud or seeds attached to it.

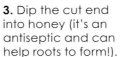

2. Remove all the leaves from the lower half of the cutting.

3. Dip the cut end into honey (it's an antiseptic and can help roots to form!).

4. Push cuttings into potting mix in a pot and firm the soil to hold it upright. Several cuttings can be put into one pot.

5. To create a warm, humid environment around the cuttings, enclose them in your mini greenhouse. Put the pot somewhere warm and bright but not in full sun. Keep moist.

6. Roots will take 4 to 6 weeks to form at which time you can repot into individual pots. After a few months when your cuttings are bigger, plant them into pretty pots for gifts.

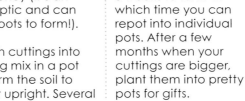

tip: Once the cuttings are growing well, remove the mini greenhouse over two weeks to expose them to stronger light in stages. The best time to take cuttings is in the warmer months when the parent plants have new growth.

You will need:

- Plant cuttings
- Small pots
- Potting mix
- Scissors
- Honey (Manuka honey is the best).
- Mini greenhouse (see Mini Greenhouse Activity)

Invisible UV Colours

Look at your garden through the eyes of a bird or insect! A mini UV (ultraviolet) torch lets you to see UV fluorescence on some flowers, some plants and even some birds at night.

NORMAL LIGHT UV LIGHT

How different these daffodils look!

Only some parts of the flower change.

Many budgerigars also fluoresce.

1. Wait until it is dark and go out into your garden with a UV mini torch. Shine the torch on flowers and foliage. You will be amazed how different many flowers look, like these daffodils.

2. You will notice that some have special hidden areas that fluoresce under UV light, such as these freesias. There are many reasons for this! Mostly it is to attract insects or birds to help with pollination.

3. Many budgerigars and parrots flouresce. Look how different this one looks under normal and UV light. Try shining a mini UV torch on lots of different things in the garden. You will be amazed at what fluoresces!

tip: A UV mini torch will show you similar colours to those in these photos. For a stronger light and for large objects, you can use a UV lamp, available from some hardware and lighting stores.

Rating: Easy

You will need:
- Mini ultraviolet torch
- Your garden flowers or fresh flowers

Planting Seeds

Seeds that you've collected or bought can be sown in the ground or pots. Biodegradable pots are ideal for fussy baby vegetables such as carrot, parsnip, parsley or beetroot. You can plant biodegradable pots with seedlings in them straight into the ground, where the pot will slowly decompose.

1. You can make your own biodegradable pots from empty toilet paper rolls.

2. You can also use an egg carton with a hole cut in the base of each to let water drain off, or you can buy a biodegradable pot from your local garden centre.

3. Fill your pot with seed-raising mix or potting mix and moisten it well. Then sow your seeds into the pot and moisten the soil again.

4. Keep on moistening the mix as the days go by. Depending on what you're growing, the seeds could take a few weeks to sprout.

5. Once they're up, keep on misting the seedlings and let them grow on for a few weeks more, moving them into a bit more sun as they get bigger. By this stage, the watering will have softened the pots.

6. When the seedlings are about 10cm tall, plant the whole pot into the soil, so the top of the pot is at soil level. If you like, gently pull apart the top edges of the soft, moistened pot to speed up its final disintegration, but don't overdo it.

tip: The best time to plant out most seedlings is spring. You can, however, plant your seeds into pots just before spring and let them start to grow on a warm, protected windowsill inside the house. By the time spring arrives you'll be ready to plant them out.

Strawberry Tower

You will be eating your own delicious strawberries in no time when you make this strawberry tower. The best time to plant is in early spring.

1. Start by almost filling the biggest pot with good quality potting mix and partly bury the smaller pot on top. There should be enough room for planting around the edge of the bigger pot.

2. Use a trowel to add more potting mix.

3. Plant strawberry plants around the edges of the big pot. You should be able to fit 3 or 4 plants in.

4. Plant some more strawberries in the smaller pot.

5. Put your name on your pot. You can have a strawberry growing competition with your siblings or friends!

6. Water your strawberry tower daily and water in a soluble fertiliser every two weeks.

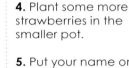

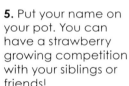

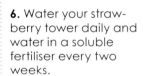

tip: *Make sure that the two pots have good drainage holes. Choose a nice sunny place to build your strawberry tower as it is heavy to move when you have finished planting. You can use plastic or ceramic pots.*

Rating: Medium

You will need:

- Two pots, one about a third bigger than the other
- Potting mix
- Strawberry plants
- Trowel

Collecting

There are wonderful treasures just lying around in home gardens. Beautiful seed pods, lush mosses, pretty flowers and seeds of all sorts of plants just waiting to be collected.

Flowers are easy and fun to collect. Our first project shows you how to collect and dry the flowers that are in your garden. Once they are dried you can make birthday or Christmas cards by gluing the dried flowers onto the cards. Or you can make works of art with the flowers which you could frame and put on your wall.

Moss is beautiful. Moss is free: it grows on pavements, on brick or stone walls, in gutters or even on the lawn in shady areas. All that you have to do is collect it and use it in moss gardens or as pretend grass around bonsai plants. Our project shows you how to do it and it is really easy.

Once you have collected your moss, our next project shows you how to create your own moss garden. Moss gardens attract pixies and fairies. If you can't find any, you can get some plastic pixies and fairies from toy shops. Or you can create any scene you like – a cricket game, a baseball or football game – or a park.

Most plants in your garden produce seeds every year. Most seeds set in late summer or early Autumn (Fall). As the green seed pods form, you can place a special bag around them to collect the seeds as they fall. Our project looks at how to get or make the seed collection bags and how to label and store the seeds until you are ready to plant them.

Wherever you live in the world, there are plants that produce amazing seed pods. Maybe there are pods left over after you have collected your seeds. Seed pods can be joined together to make cute animals or even monsters and maybe you can use some of these in your moss garden. We have special ideas in this chapter on how you make them look real and alive.

Pressing Flowers

Collect some beautiful blooms from your garden and transform them into your own floral artwork or cards for family and friends.

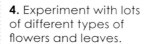

1. Collect some flowers, leaves or herbs from your garden or local area.

2. Place a piece of blotting paper or paper towels inside a heavy book. Put your flowers on top.

3. Place a piece of blotting paper or paper towel on top of your flowers. Press down gently and close the book. Putting something heavy like a brick on top of the book helps your flowers dry really flat. Leave them for about two weeks. (Thicker flowers may take longer to dry.)

4. Experiment with lots of different types of flowers and leaves.

5. Once pressed and dry, carefully remove the flowers from the paper.

6. Stick your flowers onto cardboard using PVA glue to make a giftcard or a flower picture for a frame. Use your imagination! Tip: use a paintbrush to apply the glue to the flowers.

tip: Look for flowers that aren't too chunky or thick. Daisies, pansies, violets, geraniums and leaves make good choices. Herbs like lavender or rosemary are also good choices.

Rating: Easy

You will need:
- Flowers
- Blotting paper or paper towels
- Heavy book or stack of newspapers
- Card or picture frame
- PVA glue and paint brush

Collecting Seeds

You can collect seeds from flowers, shrubs, trees, herbs and vegetables to grow your own new plants. The hunt for seeds is often the most fun of all.

1. To collect seeds you'll need to wait till the seed heads swell, mature and then release their seeds.

2. It is difficult to know exactly when seeds will be released from the flower heads, so the trick is to tie a fine mesh bag over the seed heads, to catch the seeds as they fall. Mesh bags also stop seeds being blown away on windy days, or eaten by birds or animals. We are collecting basil seeds.

3. Use a plastic twist tie to secure each bag over the seed head, and attach to the plant stem. For really fine seeds, use fine organza gift bag available from craft shops or you can sew your own from fabric. You can also use old stockings.

You will need:

- A plant that has gone to seed
- Fine mesh or organza bags
- Plastic twist tie
- Small paper bags or envelopes and a pen

4. Not all seeds are dry. Some are held inside fleshy fruit like pumpkins or tomatoes or clivia. The seed is ready to harvest when the fruit is ripe. It can be cut open and the seeds put on paper towel to dry. Seeds take about 7 to 14 days to dry in a warm, protected spot.

5. Some seeds are held in pods, like peas and beans. Leave the pods on the plant until they begin to brown. Remove the pods and allow to dry for a week, before splitting the pods open to remove the seeds inside.

6. Paper bags or envelopes are ideal for storing your collected seeds. Label each pack and include a date and store them in a cool, dry place. Use the seeds as soon as possible, as the fresher the seed, the better the chances of them growing.

tip: Once you have collected seeds, see how to sow and grow them in the Planting Seeds Activity.

Tree Creatures

Make your own leafy creatures using sticks and leaves from the garden. You can make whatever animal you like. We chose to make little birds.

1. Gather together what you need. We chose leaves with different textures and colours.

2. Make the body with cotton wool folded inside a piece of foil (you could also use florist's foam).

3. Fold and squish the foil into a small bird shape. Tip: it might take a couple of attempts to get it right!

4. Lightly glue on leaves and twigs to form feathers, then attach buds and nuts for eyes and tail feathers. Use craft glue or a hot glue gun, just don't use too much of either. Tip: always supervise children using hot glue guns.

5. Twist some pipe cleaners to make the legs and feet. Fine gauge copper wire also works well.

6. Birds can be wired or twisted onto a branch outside or on indoor plants to welcome guests!

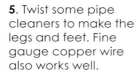

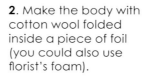

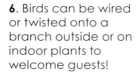

tip: Kids can forage in the garden, nature strip or a local park for leaves with interesting shapes and textures (small is best), and some flower buds, seed heads, fallen nuts or cones.

Rating: Medium

You will need:

- Seed heads
- Leaves, sticks and nuts
- Cotton wool
- Aluminium foil
- Craft glue or hot glue gun
- Pipe cleaners or wire for feet

Collecting Moss

Go on a fun adventure hunting for moss and collect it for your projects. As long as you keep it moist and in the shade, it will store well until you're ready to use it.

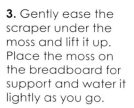

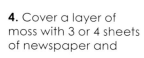

1. Collect what you will need.

2. Go looking around your neighbourhood for moss in damp spots in the lawn or concrete paths, on road gutters or footpaths.

3. Gently ease the scraper under the moss and lift it up. Place the moss on the breadboard for support and water it lightly as you go.

4. Cover a layer of moss with 3 or 4 sheets of newspaper and lay another layer of moss on top. Three to five layers of moss is enough: more than that may fall over.

5. It's best to use the moss straight away – however, the layered board can be used to store moss for up to 3 days prior to use.

6. Even better, once you get home, is to re-lay the moss in a shady area, one layer thick prior to watering it. This will enable you to use the moss over several weeks if necessary.

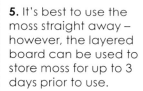

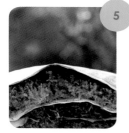

tip: Your collected moss can be used to make the Living Moss Garden, the Miniature Garden or the Bonsai projects in this book.

Rating: Medium

You will need:
- Paint scraper or spatula
- Old plastic breadboard or similar
- Bottle of water
- Newspaper

Living Moss Garden

There's nothing quite like moss. It's the most beautiful shade of green and it feels amazing to touch. You can easily make a living moss garden. As long as you give it a regular spray with water, it will live happily in your room for months.

1. Collect some moss. You'll need enough to cover an average sized chopping board (see Collecting Moss Activity).

2. You'll also need various decorations; we used an old tree branch, pebbles, bird and butterfly decorations and some bead letters.

3. Place your old tree branch in the middle of the dish and use a trowel to surround it with some damp potting mix or soil making a little hill in the middle.

4. Add your moss, lay it in neatly like carpet until the soil is covered.

5. Use whatever decorations you like to theme your moss garden, we used some pebbles and plastic butterflies bought from the local craft shop, as well as a little metal bird and wood letters from the bargain shop.

6. Once you are happy with your design give it a spray with some water and enjoy. Experiment with different themes and objects for a different look.

> **tip:** *Moss does best outdoors in a semi-shaded position. Keep your indoor moss garden near the window and give it a holiday outdoors in a semi-shaded position if it starts to die off.*

Rating: Medium

You will need:

- Moss
- Shallow dish
- Potting mix or soil
- Old tree branch
- Pebbles
- Decorations
- Trowel

MOSS

Making and Creating

This chapter is choc-a-block full of things that you can make yourself. These are fun ideas that are perfect for weekends or during school holidays.

Why not make crazy creatures like a green, hairy caterpillar that grows. You can also make a Pot Plant Family: pots with faces painted on them and growing plants that look like hair.

Or perhaps you'd like to grow a terrarium. You can create a world in miniature with living plants inside an old fishbowl or aquarium.

One really interesting project is where you change the colour of flowers. With food colouring you can change a white flower into a yellow one or into some other colour.

Or maybe your vegetable garden needs a scarecrow. We have a project where you make a scarecrow from old bits and pieces.

If you like bonsai or Japanese miniature trees, we'll show you how to get started There are other projects where you grow succulent plants in colourful old shoes, plus some ideas for city dwellers.

There is also a project on how to design a complete garden from scratch. This is a simple project when you use cut-out drawings (icons) of the things that you may want in your garden.

Egg Head

These 'eggheads' with hair made from cress seedlings look cute, and the tips can be harvested and added to sandwiches and salads.
It's a quick and easy way to grow something edible.

1. Collect what you will need. Look for cute eggcups, they make this project even more fun.

2. Put a small amount of moist potting mix in the bottom half of the eggshell.

3. Place two or three cotton wool balls on top.

4. Sprinkle on some cress seeds, about 1/4 teaspoon of seeds per egg is enough.

5. Water seeds in with a small cup to moisten the cotton wool, trying not to flood the shells.

6. Place your eggheads on a well-lit windowsill. Keep them moist but do not flood them. As seedlings begin to germinate, rotate the eggheads a quarter turn every day for even growth all round. Displaying them in eggcups looks great and keeps them upright.

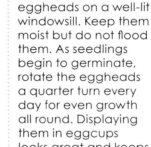

> **tip:** You can use cress seeds or alfalfa seeds. A spray bottle is a handy way to water the eggheads. Once you've harvested all the leaves put the eggshells and soil in the compost heap.

Rating: Easy

You will need:

- Empty eggshells
- Cotton wool balls
- Potting mix
- Packet of cress seeds
- Eggcups

Pot Plant Family

What fun to create your own pot plant people with curly hair
that just keeps growing! You will need to trim their hair yourself! You can make large
or smaller pots and have a whole family in your garden.

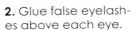

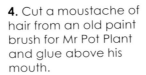

1. Paste on the eyes using two blobs of craft glue in the position where you would like them. Stick the eyes on.

2. Glue false eyelashes above each eye.

3. Paint a mouth and nose on each pot. Make one mouth bright red so that it looks like lipstick for Mrs or Miss Pot Plant.

4. Cut a moustache of hair from an old paint brush for Mr Pot Plant and glue above his mouth.

5. When the glue and paint is dry, paint both pots on the inside and outside with a sealant. Allow to dry before planting.

6. Put some potting mix into the bottom of each pot and then plant the corkscrew rush. Fill the pots with potting mix and water well. This pot plant family have hair that just keeps on growing!

tip: You may like to try other plants like mondo grass (Ophiopogon), or other rushes (Acorus) or grass-like plants.

Rating: Easy

You will need:
- Two terracotta pots
- Craft glue
- Eyes and false eyelashes from craft shop
- Paint
- Old paint brush
- Terracotta pot sealant
- Potting mix
- Two corkscrew rush, *Juncus effusus 'Spiralis'* plants

Succulent Sculptures

Succulents are such tough plants they even grow in pure sand. Make some really colourful sand cups using old plastic tumblers and give your succulents a bright happy home.

1. Collect what you will need and visit a nursery to buy a selection of succulents (we used *Sempervivum tectorum*, mixed *Echeverias* and *Echeveria* 'Black Prince').

2. Ask an adult to drill two holes in the bottom of each cup, to let water drain out; put a square of mesh in the bottom so that sand does not wash away.

3. Scoop in a few layers of coloured sand and/or pebbles, to fill the cup up to about half-way.

4. Remove the succulent plant from its plastic pot and rinse off the excess soil from the roots.

5. Plant the succulent into the cup, making sure that the bottom set of leaves is above the rim of the cup. Fill up the cup with sand or pebbles using a trowel and a funnel.

6. Put a few cups together so they look nice and keep them on a sunny windowsill, or outside. Water weekly.

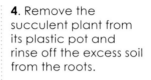

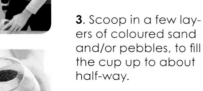

tip: *Succulents love:* • *Lots of sunshine* • *Being outside* • *Being with other succulents* • *And not too much rain or water!*

Rating: Medium

You will need:
- Clear plastic tumblers
- Cordless drill
- Plastic funnel
- Colourful sand
- Colourful small pebbles
- Succulents
- Trowel

Make a Scarecrow

Scarecrows are used to scare birds away from your vegetable patch so they don't eat your crops. Even if you don't grow vegetables they are a cool addition to your garden!

1. Collect what you will need. Choose clothes appropriate for the size you want your scarecrow to be.

2. Sew the shirt to the waist of the trousers. This gives a 'skin' into which you can stuff straw or filling. Ask a parent to assist you.

3. Use some string to tie off the straw feet at the bottom of your scarecrow's trousers. You can also use a length of rope as a belt to hold up pants.

4. Fill the pillowcase, which will become the head, with straw or stuffing and tie off

with a rubber band, or if using a piece of material then pile straw in the middle and draw corners up to form a ball and tie off. Paint a face on the head.

5. Take the two garden stakes and hammer together or tie with wire to form a cross. Find a good spot in the garden and hammer the vertical stake into the ground. Ask a parent to assist you.

6. Put the head over the vertical garden stake and then tie the scarecrow to the horizontal stake. Put on his hat.

tip: Search on the internet for some photos of scarecrows to get other ideas and inspiration. You'll be amazed at what can be created.

Rating: Medium

You will need:

- old clothes, gloves, hat
- old pillowcase or material
- needle and thread
- rubber band
- straw and/or stuffing
- paint and paint brush
- string or rope
- 2 x garden stakes
- hammer and nails or wire.

Miniature Garden

Terrariums are a miniature garden in a jar! Create your own and enjoy for months.

1. Collect what you need. Your container should be large enough to put your hands in for planting, and tall enough to suit your choice of plants. Fishbowls are perfect.

2. Use a trowel to fill the base of the container with a layer of small gravel or pebbles for drainage.

3. Add some quality potting mix, enough to accommodate the roots of chosen plants, around 3-5cm deep. You can add a little more later to cover the roots.

4. Plant tall plants like parlour palms in the centre, or at the back, then surround with smaller plants such as dichondra and moss or baby's tears as ground cover.

5. Add some coloured pebbles and decorate to create a theme. We chose butterflies and horses.

6. Lightly mist the container with water from a spray bottle each day. Don't overdo it, as there are no drainage holes. Keep it moist but not wet.

> **tip:** *Terrariums make condensation that drips down the inside to water the plants, requiring very little additional water. See Collecting Moss for moss tips! You may need to reduce the root mass of your plants so they fit. To do this, tease out the roots with your fingers and trim with scissors.*

Rating: Medium

You will need:

- A clear glass or plastic container
- Gravel
- Potting mix
- Plants
- Mist spray bottle
- Coloured pebbles
- Decorations
- Trowel

Changing Flower Colours

You can change white flowers into almost any colour you like overnight. This simple trick will allow you to turn flowers into colours even Mother Nature can't match!

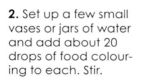

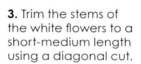

1. Collect together what you will need. The flowers should be fresh for this project to work well.

2. Set up a few small vases or jars of water and add about 20 drops of food colouring to each. Stir.

3. Trim the stems of the white flowers to a short-medium length using a diagonal cut.

4. The diagonal cut allows the coloured water to be taken up via the stem to the flowers more easily.

(The flower will suck up the liquid and turn that colour).

5. Place a few flowers in each jar of coloured water and leave overnight.

6. When you wake up, the flowers will have absorbed the food colouring and changed colour! Remove flowers from coloured water and display in a vase of fresh water.

tip: Experiment by mixing different food colouring drops together in your vase. Red and blue make purple. Yellow and red make orange. Invent your own colours!

You will need:

- White flowers such as carnations or daisies
- Clear plastic glasses or vases
- Food colouring
- Water
- Scissors

Hairy Caterpillars & Snakes

Create a caterpillar or snake indoors on a windowsill and watch them grow.

1. Fill a small section of the stocking with a small amount of moist potting mix, starting at the toe.

2. Stretch the stocking open and start to sprinkle grass seed along the side. For the grassy snake, add potting mix and a small handful of seed along one side of the stocking.

3. To shape the caterpillar, tie filled and seeded sections off in a knot, or fasten with rubber bands. Continue to place seed, potting mix and knot in sections along the length of the stocking. Do not put seed in the first toe section or you will get grass on the face.

4. Tie off the sections with ribbon or a rubber band.

5. Add pipe cleaners for feelers and old buttons, badges or bottle caps for eyes.

6. Spray with water to thoroughly moisten and sit it in a saucer on a well-lit windowsill. Keep moist, and within 10 days, the grass germinates. As it grows you can trim.

tip: *Rotate the snake or caterpillar every day or two as it germinates, as the grass will grow towards the sunlight. Rotating will help the grass grow evenly.*

You will need:

- Grass seed
- Potting mix
- Old stocking or thin sock
- Buttons
- Pipe cleaners
- Ribbon

Seedpod Aliens

Get creative and make aliens and little monsters from the seedpods that you collect in your garden or local park. They make great gifts or decorations.

1. Gather whatever seedpods you can find. We used acorns and gumnuts. Also gather your craft items.

2. Take a double acorn cap and glue a large pom pom into one of the caps.

3. Glue an eye to each of two small pom poms.

4. Glue the small pom poms with eyes onto the large pom pom.

5. Take a feather and either tuck it into the acorn cap behind the pom pom or glue it on.

6. Cut a pipecleaner in half and twist around the acorn to make arms. We made lots of aliens to play together and displayed them in a saucer of gritty sand that looks like the surface of an alien planet.

tip: Experiment using different seedpods and craft items to make unique aliens and monsters. Make some with friends and see how many little monsters you can invent!

You will need:

- Seedpods
- Craft glue or glue gun
- Large and small pom poms
- Coloured pipecleaners and feathers
- Stick on eyes

Succulent Shoes

Succulents look really interesting and are easy to grow. They are so tough they will even grow in old shoes! We painted our shoes bright colours and used lots of different types of succulents.

1. Collect some old shoes. If the shoes are a boring colour, paint them with shoe paint. Allow a day for them to dry.

2. Ask an adult to drill holes in the soles for drainage. Put in at least three good holes in each shoe.

3. Using a trowel, fill shoes with some free-draining (or succulent) potting mix. You can make a paper funnel so it's easier to get the potting mix into the shoes.

4. Plant your succulents into the shoes. We used *Echeveria*, *Kalanchoe*, *Sedum* 'Jelly Bean' and *Sempervivum tectorum*.

5. They need very little water so use a small cup to pour water into the shoes. Test the soil every week with your finger and when the soil feels dry it is time to water them again.

6. Display your shoes in the garden or on steps near the house.

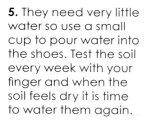

tip: Succulents do not like to be in soggy soil so be sure to use free draining potting mix for succulents and make sure you ask an adult to drill drainage holes in your old shoes before you plant.

You will need:

- Old shoes
- Drill
- Shoe paint
- Succulent potting mix
- Succulents (plants)
- Small watering cup
- Trowel

Make a Bonsai

Bonsai is the traditional Japanese art of creating miniature trees in containers. You can make your own bonsai from many types of plants.

1. It's best to ask your local nursery or bonsai nursery to help you choose a suitable plant and pot for it. They can also help with tools. We used a juniper and chose a pot that would measure about two-thirds the height of the plant.

2. Find the thickest branches on the plant that will be kept and cut off the thinnest branches and any small shoots and excess leaves.

Decide which is the front and back of your bonsai.

3. Take the thicker 2mm aluminium wire, and cut it one third longer than the height of the plant. Push one end into the soil at the base of the trunk and wind it around the trunk to the top. Trim excess wire at the top.

tip: There are many different shapes you can choose for your bonsai. We made the 'Informal Upright' or Moyogi which is a triangular shape where the trunk is upright and bent in an 'S' shape with branching at each turn.

Rating: Tricky

You will need:
- Plant to bonsai
- Tools: scissors, pliers, wire cutter, small fork, chopsticks
- Bonsai pot with drainage holes
- Bonsai potting mix
- Drainage mesh
- Aluminium wire, 1.5mm and 2mm gauge
- Moss and pebbles
- Trowel

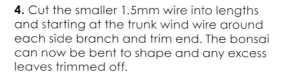

4. Cut the smaller 1.5mm wire into lengths and starting at the trunk wind wire around each side branch and trim end. The bonsai can now be bent to shape and any excess leaves trimmed off.

5. Place the mesh in the base of your pot to cover drainage holes. Cut a length of 1.5mm wire 6cm longer than the pot and insert it from the outside through the drainage holes evenly. Half fill the pot with potting mix, mounding it in the centre.

6. Remove bonsai from pot and use a fork to tease the soil out of the roots. Trim roots by about one-third and place bonsai off centre in the pot with the roots over the soil mound. Fill with potting mix pressing down firmly with fingers and twist together the wire at the back of the plant burying the ends. This will stabilise the bonsai in the pot.

7. Spray the potting mix with water until moist. Add moss around the trunk of the bonsai and then pebbles around the edge. This makes it look old and helps retain moisture.

tip: *There's a lot to learn about Bonsai. Some gardeners have been creating bonsai for all their life! Try to find a Bonsai course near you to find out more and keep practicing!*

City living

If you live in an apartment or flat in the city and don't have a garden, don't despair! Many of the projects in this book can be done indoors or placed on a windowsill.

Perfect apartment activities:

- **Pressing Flowers**
- **Miniature Garden**
- **Hairy Caterpillar**
- **Egg Head**
- **Seedpod Aliens**
- **Leaf Creatures**
- **Succulent Sculpture**
- **Changing Flower Colours**

1-2. Why not visit your local park to collect seeds and seedpods for some of the projects and explore!

3. Team up with some friends and create a mini garden in a pot or window box. Herbs are great in pots and easy to grow.

If you have a windowsill or balcony you can keep your mini garden there. You can replace the herbs as the seasons change.

Garden Planner

You can plan your own dream garden. We have made a landscape kit for you on our website. Type in the link below and you will be able to print out two A4 pages of landscaping icons plus a sheet of grid paper to create your own garden.

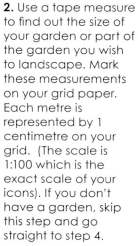

1. Go to the link below on your computer and print our Kids Landscape Kit. Cut out the garden icons.

2. Use a tape measure to find out the size of your garden or part of the garden you wish to landscape. Mark these measurements on your grid paper. Each metre is represented by 1 centimetre on your grid. (The scale is 1:100 which is the exact scale of your icons). If you don't have a garden, skip this step and go straight to step 4.

3. Use a compass to work out north, mark it on your grid. This will tell you where the sunny and shady spots are in your garden.

4. Arrange your icons on the grid paper. Move them around until you have a design you are happy with.

5. Once you are happy with your positioning, glue the icons down.

6. You can print off as many kits as you like.

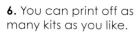

link:
www.burkesbackyard.com.au/kidslandscapekit.pdf

Rating: Medium

You will need:
• Computer and colour printer
• Paper
• Scissors
• Tape measure
• Compass
• Glue

cubby house

BIKE GARDEN

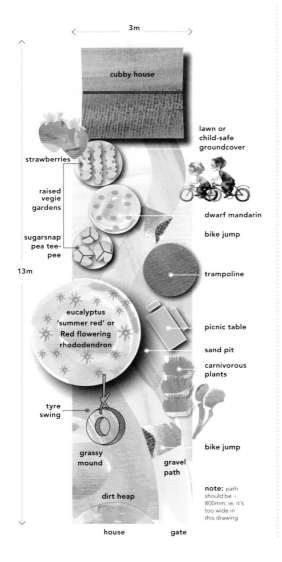

3m

cubby house

lawn or child-safe groundcover

strawberries

raised vegie gardens

sugarsnap pea tee-pee

dwarf mandarin

bike jump

13m

trampoline

eucalyptus 'summer red' or Red flowering rhododendron

picnic table

sand pit

carnivorous plants

tyre swing

grassy mound

gravel path

bike jump

dirt heap

note: path should be ~ 800mm; ie, it's too wide in this drawing

house   gate

FAIRY GARDEN

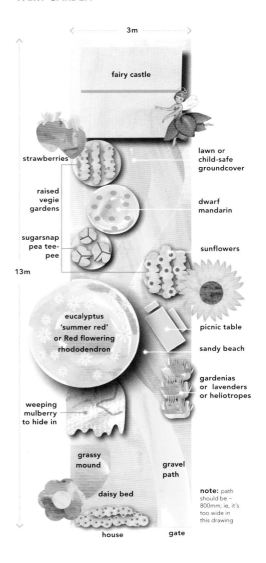

3m

fairy castle

lawn or child-safe groundcover

strawberries

raised vegie gardens

dwarf mandarin

sugarsnap pea tee-pee

sunflowers

13m

eucalyptus 'summer red' or Red flowering rhododendron

picnic table

sandy beach

gardenias or lavenders or heliotropes

weeping mulberry to hide in

grassy mound

gravel path

daisy bed

note: path should be ~ 800mm; ie, it's too wide in this drawing

house   gate

International Seed Suppliers

Seeds for the plants used in this book are available
all around the world.
Most nurseries will stock them.
Dwarf Snapdragons (*Antirrhinum*) and Nasturtiums
are available from the following seed suppliers.

UK and EU countries:

Unwins
www.unwins.co.uk
Unwins, Alconbury Hill,
Huntingdon, PE28 4HY

Thompson & Morgan
www.thompson-morgan.
com
Poplar Lane, Ipswich.
Suffolk IP8 3BU

Marshalls
S E Marshall & Co
www.marshalls-seeds.co.uk
Alconbury Hill, Huntingdon,
Cambs, PE28 4HY

USA:

Burpee Seeds
www.burpee.com
W. Atlee Burpee & Co.
300 Park Avenue
Warminster, PA 18974

Harris Seeds
www.harrisseeds.com
355 Paul Road
P.O. Box 24966
Rochester, NY 14624-0966

AUSTRALIA:

Mr Fothergill's
www.mrfothergills-seeds-
bulbs.com.au
15B Walker Street
South Windsor NSW 2756

Eden Seeds
www.edenseeds.com.au
M.S. 905, Lower Beechmont
QLD 4211

The Diggers Club
www.diggers.com.au
PO Box 300,
Dromana VIC 3936

Yates
www.yates.com.au
Available at nurseries,
garden centres.
Location of nearest retailer
can be found on website.

This edition published in 2014 by
Reed New Holland an imprint of New Holland Publishers (Australia) Pty Ltd
London • Sydney • Auckland

The Chandlery Unit 114 50 Westminster Bridge Road London SE1 7QY United Kingdom
1/66 Gibbes Street Chatswood NSW 2067 Australia
218 Lake Road Northcote Auckland New Zealand

www.newhollandpublishers.com

A record of this book is held at the National Library of Australia

ISBN 9781921517464

Publisher: Fiona Schultz
Publishing director: Lliane Clarke
Designers: Kimberley Pearce, Tracy Loughlin
Production director: Olga Dementiev
Printer: Toppan Leefung Printing (China)

Author: Don Burke
Horticultural Consultants: Elizabeth Swane and Jenny James
Burke's Backyard Creative Director: Zora Regulic
Burke's Backyard Art Director: Kim Gregory
Producer: Chris Burke
Principal Photography: Brent Wilson
New York photography: Seán van Doornum

With thanks to: Megumi Bennett www.megumibennettbonsai.com, Ben Hewett, Jamie McIlwraith, Ed Coyle, and Julie McCrory.
Our biggest most sincere thanks to all the kids who helped us with these projects: Matt and Luke Carrah, Sophie Crookshanks, Isabella
D'Antionio, Paris and Harry Le Boursicot, Tom Nowland, Cassidy McCrory, Isabella Napthali
Georgina Trotter, Riley Vidulich, Grace Waters, Jack & Leah Westoll, Hamish & Curtis Wood, and Kellan, Ezio and Esme in New York City.

Keep up with New Holland Publishers on Facebook
www.facebook.com/NewHollandPublishers